It's Jesus' Birthday!

A Christmas Eve Service

Cynthia E. Cowen

CSS Publishing Company, Inc., Lima, Ohio

IT'S JESUS' BIRTHDAY!

ISBN 0-7880-1063-8

PRINTED IN U.S.A.

"A friend loves at all times," Proverbs 17:17 states. "Some friends play at friendship but a true friend sticks closer than one's nearest kin," says the writer of Proverbs 18:24. I have been blessed in my life with many special friends who exemplify these two proverbs, but two in particular I would like to single out. And so, I dedicate this resource to my dear friends, Linda Kitzman and Ann Johnson. Both of these women take me as I am. They listen, encourage, and support me in my ministries. They give love unconditionally and are available even though both are active in their vocations, churches, and communities. Both stick close in the ups and downs of our lives. They are "kin" in Christ and for that I am truly blessed with my wonderful "sisters" in Jesus.

Cynthia E. Cowen

It's Jesus' Birthday!

Christmas Eve

*Call To Worship
P: Come, it's Jesus' birthday! Come, let us go to the stable of Bethlehem! Come, let us worship Christ, the newborn King!

*Opening Hymn: "Oh, Come, All Ye Faithful"
>Oh, come, all ye faithful, joyful and triumphant!
>Oh, come ye, oh, come ye to Bethlehem;
>Come and behold him, born the king of angels:

>Refrain: Oh, come, let us adore him,
>Oh, come, let us adore him,
>Oh, come, let us adore him, Christ the Lord!

>The highest, most holy, Light of light eternal,
>Born of a virgin, a mortal he comes;
>Son of the Father, now in flesh appearing! Refrain

>Sing, choirs of angels, Sing in exultation,
>Sing, all ye citizens of heaven above!
>Glory to God, in the highest: Refrain

We Celebrate The Birth Of Jesus

*P: As the angels announced the birth of the Savior,
C: We celebrate the birth of our Lord Jesus!
P: The heavens declare the glory of God;
C: We proclaim good tidings of joy to all people!
P: The shepherds ran to a Bethlehem stable to see a babe lying in the manger.

C: **We come today to worship the Christ child born anew in our hearts and lives.**

P: We rejoice in the new life God gives us as we await Christ's coming again.

C: **Come into our lives and our world, Lord Jesus.**

P: The shepherds praised and worshiped God for all they had seen and heard.

C: **We praise and worship you, Almighty God, for the birth of your Son, Jesus, born to us once more and placed in the mangers of our hearts. Amen.**

*Hymn: "Away In A Manger"

> Away in a manger, no crib for his bed,
> The little Lord Jesus laid down his sweet head.
> The stars in the sky looked down where he lay,
> The little Lord Jesus asleep on the hay.
>
> The cattle are lowing; the poor baby wakes,
> But little Lord Jesus, no crying he makes.
> I love you, Lord Jesus; look down from the sky
> And stay by my cradle till morning is nigh.
>
> Be near me, Lord Jesus; I ask you to stay
> Close by me forever and love me, I pray.
> Bless all the dear children in your tender care
> And fit us for heaven to live with you there.

The Word Proclaims The Birth Of Jesus

First Reading: Isaiah 9:2-7

Cherub and Junior Choirs and/or Bells

Responsive Christmas Litany (Based on Psalm 96)

P: Sing to the Lord a new song; sing to the Lord, all the earth!

C: **We sing praise to Christ, the newborn King!**

P: As we sing praise to the name of the Lord and proclaim God's salvation, let us declare the glory of the Lord and God's marvelous deeds among all peoples.

C: **The Lord is great and worthy of praise, for he gave us his Son, our Lord Jesus.**

P: The heavens display God's splendor and majesty; God's strength and glory are seen in his sanctuary.

C: **Glory to God in the highest; glory to the name of Jesus, God's Son.**

P: We worship the Lord in the splendor of God's holiness; all the earth trembles before the Lord our God.

C: **We kneel before the manger and behold the Christ child who will be our righteous judge.**

P: The heavens rejoice! The earth is glad! The fields and their creatures, yes, the trees and birds, all sing for joy!

C: **We sing joy to the Lord, who comes to judge the world in righteousness and truth.**

Hymn: "Joy To The World"
Joy to the world, the Lord is come!
Let earth receive its King;
Let ev'ry heart prepare him room,
And heav'n and nature sing,
And heav'n and nature sing,
And heav'n, and heav'n and nature sing.

He rules the world with truth and grace,
And makes the nations prove
The glories of his righteousness,
And wonders of his love,
And wonders of his love,
And wonders, wonders of his love.

Second Reading: Titus 2:11-14

7

The Gospel Proclaims The Birth Of Christ

*Hymn: "What Child Is This?"
> What child is this, who, laid to rest,
> On Mary's lap is sleeping?
> Whom angels greet with anthems sweet
> While shepherds watch are keeping?
> This, this is Christ the king,
> Whom shepherds guard and angels sing;
> Haste, haste to bring him laud,
> The babe, the son of Mary!

*The Christmas Gospel: Luke 2:1-20

*Hymn: "What Child Is This?"
> Why lies he in such mean estate
> Where ox and ass are feeding?
> Good Christian, fear; for sinners here
> The silent Word is pleading.
> Nails, spear shall pierce him through,
> The cross be borne for me, for you;
> Hail, hail the Word made flesh,
> The babe, the son of Mary!

Come To The Party! — Skit and message

Hymn: "Silent Night"
> Silent night, holy night!
> All is calm, all is bright
> Round yon virgin mother and child.
> Holy Infant, so tender and mild,
> Sleep in heavenly peace,
> Sleep in heavenly peace.
>
> Silent night, holy night!
> Shepherds quake at the sight;
> Glories stream from heaven afar,

Heav'nly hosts sing Alleluia!
Christ, the Savior, is born!
Christ, the Savior, is born!

Silent night, holy night!
Son of God, love's pure light;
Radiant beams from your holy face
With the dawn of redeeming grace,
Jesus, Lord, at your birth,
Jesus, Lord, at your birth.

We Proclaim The Birth Of Christ In Today's World

Offering

Offertory: Christmas Hymn Set

Hymn: "It Came Upon The Midnight Clear"
It came upon the midnight clear,
That glorious song of old,
From angels bending near the earth
To touch their harps of gold:
"Peace on the earth, good will to all,
From heav'n's all-gracious king."
The world in solemn stillness lay
To hear the angels sing.

Still through the cloven skies they come
With peaceful wings unfurled,
And still their heav'nly music floats
O'er all the weary world.
Above its sad and lowly plains
They bend on hov'ring wing.
And ever o'er its babel sounds
The blessed angels sing.

Hymn: "Angels, From the Realms of Glory"
Angels, from the realms of glory,
Wing your flight o'er all the earth;
Once you sang creation's story;
Now proclaim Messiah's birth:

Refrain: Come and worship, come and worship,
Worship Christ, the newborn king.

Shepherds, in the fields abiding,
Watching o'er your flocks by night,
God with us is now residing,
Yonder shines the infant light. Refrain

Solo — "O Holy Night"

Hymn: "Hark! The Herald Angels Sing"
Hark! The herald angels sing,
"Glory to the newborn king;
Peace on earth, and mercy mild,
God and sinners reconciled."
Joyful, all you nations, rise;
Join the triumph of the skies;
With angelic hosts proclaim,
"Christ is born in Bethlehem!"

Refrain: Hark! The herald angels sing,
"Glory to the newborn king!"

Hail the heav'n-born Prince of Peace!
Hail the sun of righteousness!
Light and life to all he brings,
Ris'n with healing in his wings.
Mild he lays his glory by,
Born that we no more may die,
Born to raise each child of earth,
Born to give us second birth. Refrain

*Prayers Of The Church

P: Dear God, the message of salvation is proclaimed tonight in the birth of your Son, our Lord Jesus. Give us ears to hear the Good News and feet ready to run like the shepherds to tell others about your love found in a manger and hung on a cross.

C: **Hear our prayer, Holy Jesus.**

P: Advent has been a time of waiting, of preparation. As Mary was prepared for the birth of Jesus, you have prepared us to celebrate his birth once again. Help us to be faithful as we prepare for your coming again.

C: **Hear our prayer, Holy Jesus.**

P: Like Mary and Joseph, we are a people making our way to Bethlehem, making our way toward Christmas. However, we cannot celebrate Christmas without ever encountering the Christ Child. Forgive us for putting other things before you, Lord Jesus. Confront us with our need for a savior.

C: **Hear our prayer, Holy Jesus.**

P: We kneel at the manger and gaze upon your small body with love, Infant Jesus. We stand at the Cross and look upon your body broken and your blood shed for us in love, Savior of the World. Use our bodies as you did Mary's to house your Holy Spirit. Use our lips as you did hers in obedience to your will for our lives. Use our hands as you did hers to care for those around us. Use our feet as you did hers to follow where you lead.

C: **Hear our prayer, Holy Jesus.**

P: Lord Jesus, we remember those in our midst who are sick, grieving, lonely, especially those we name before you now or in the silence of our hearts. *(Petitions may be offered up.)* Be with them and bring them healing, comfort, and your tender and gentle presence.

C: **Hear our prayer, Holy Jesus.**

P: We remember tonight our troops throughout the world who celebrate your birth away from family and friends. Connect them in love to the body of Christ as they worship this night wherever they may find themselves. Be with them and bring peace to all nations.

C: **Hear our prayer, Holy Jesus.**

P: We stand on this silent and holy night free to begin again, forgiven and forgiving people, unafraid to proclaim you as Lord. May our hearts beat as one with you, Child of Bethlehem, as we go forth declaring your glory and your promise of peace in our hearts.

C: **Glory to you, Holy Jesus, and peace to all people on earth! Amen.**

*The Lord's Prayer

Our Father, who art in heaven,
hallowed be thy name,
thy kingdom come,
thy will be done,
on earth as it is in heaven.
Give us this day our daily bread;
and forgive us our trespasses,
as we forgive those
who trespass against us;
and lead us not into temptation,
but deliver us from evil.
For thine is the kingdom,
and the power, and the glory,
forever and ever. Amen.

*Benediction

P: Go in the name of Jesus whose birth we celebrate tonight. Go in the love of God who sent His Son, our Savior. Go in the power of the Holy Spirit, proclaiming by your life this wondrous news.

C: **We go celebrating Jesus, our Lord and our Savior. We go celebrating Christ in our lives! Amen.**

*Closing Hymn: "Go Tell It On The Mountain"

Refrain: Go tell it on the mountain,
Over the hills and ev'rywhere;
Go tell it on the mountain
That Jesus Christ is born!

While shepherds kept their watching
O'er silent flocks by night,
Behold, throughout the heavens
There shone a holy light. Refrain

The shepherds feared and trembled
When, lo, above the earth
Rang out the angel chorus
That hailed our Savior's birth. Refrain

Down in a lonely manger
The humble Christ was born;
And God sent us salvation
That blessed Christmas morn. Refrain

Come To The Party!

Participants: Leah, innkeeper's wife; Jacob, the innkeeper; son; pastor

Leah, the innkeeper's wife: "Hurry up, Leah, get that bed changed!" "Come on, Leah, I need that room swept, pronto!" "Leah! More food for our guests!" That was all I was hearing lately from my husband, and it was beginning to take its toll on me. Oh, oh, I better get busy. Here comes my husband, Jacob, the innkeeper.

Jacob, the innkeeper: *(Enters and takes a seat. Counts his money gleefully.)*

Leah: Jacob thinks our Bethlehem Inn is a four star hotel. And it is, but only because of me! I'm his wife, Leah, and the only maid here. I work, and he profits. Just look at him counting up his money. All he sees is that gold coin coming into his pockets, thanks to that census Caesar Augustus ordered. Census ... that's taking a count, you know. I could do that. In fact, I need a break, so I'm going to take my own census right now. Let me see how many children we have here tonight ... 1, 2, 3, 4 ... Oh, this is harder than I thought. How about you children helping me by coming up here while I sit down in my chair? *(Motions children to come up.)* That's right, come right up here so I can get a better head count. *(Travel music played while children come down.)* My, don't you all look nice tonight. You're a lot better looking than me. You're all dressed up, and I have my cleaning clothes on. Is this a special night for you? *(Let children respond.)* What is Christmas? Oh ... so this night is the night you celebrate somebody's birthday?

Jacob: *(Rises and comes over to the group.)* Birthday? Did I hear somebody say they're celebrating a birthday? Leah, did you clear that with me? You know every available space is taken here at our Bethlehem Inn. There's no room for a birthday party. No, no, children. There's no room for a party like that. You'd better go home. And, you, my dear wife, had better get back to work. *(Begins to leave, jiggling his money bag.)* Oh, look! Here comes another customer. *(Waves them away.)* Sorry, mister, there's no room in this inn. Try the Super 8 down on Nazareth Street!

Leah: No, kids, you don't have to go. Jacob's just got his mind set on other things right now. This season has gotten him focused on one thing alone — making a buck from other folks' needs. Did you know he even made money off that poor couple he sent down to the stable? And the man's wife was expecting her first baby, they told me. Babies are so precious that we celebrate the day they are born with a birthday party. We celebrate a gift of life. And did you know that gift of life came to that young couple? Little does my husband know that we had a birthday party just this night. What a party it was, with guests and all! And do you know where that party happened? Right in the stable behind our inn. Yep, that young girl, Mary was her name, gave birth to a baby boy. Her husband Joseph came and asked me to help. Now don't tell Jacob I took time to go and help them out. Mary needed me more than the other guests did. And she was a real trouper as she gave birth to that gift of life. And you know what she named him? Jesus — his name means "one who saves." I took some clothes I had from our extra linen pile because I knew they wouldn't have any — they looked so poor. I wrapped that baby up in them and put him in a manger. You see, there was no bed down in that stable. But the clean hay made a warm cradle. What a gift of life Mary presented to the world. But then you know what happened? Well, a whole bunch of shepherds appeared at the door and wanted to come in and see the baby! Well, it turned out to be a birthday party — a birthday party for Jesus! After seeing him, the shepherds were so filled with joy and excitement that they ran to tell others about this baby Jesus. I'm feeling so good right now that I want to share my joy and happiness of tonight with you. I know this isn't your birthday, but I want to give you a gift to celebrate Jesus' birthday.

I'm sharing my gift with you because, like the shepherds, I want to spread this night's celebration. But the greatest gift I could give you is the gift that would help you to be touched by Jesus, because when he touches your life, you, too, will want to share gifts and help others to know Jesus, the gift of life. Shall we pray? Lord God, we thank you for the gift of these precious children who have come here tonight to celebrate the birth of your Son Jesus. Look with favor upon them and their families gathered here to worship the Christ Child. Help them to grow in wisdom and understanding of who you are. Hold them close to your heart and increase their love for you and others. Touch them this night, we pray. Amen.

Look! Here comes my son to help me clean. I bet he can help me give out my gifts, and then you can return to your seat. *(Lad enters and helps distribute candy or other gift item.)*

Pastor's Reflection
Pastor: Leah, our innkeeper's wife, summed up the whole meaning of Christmas, didn't she? Christmas is a celebration of the gift of life, a baby born, a child taking his first breath, and all the hope that this new life brings and gives to a family. But this gift of life has turned everything all around because Jesus came not to receive but to give — to give the very thing which we celebrate tonight — his life. And what a gift that is!

Because he was born as a child in a stable, behind an inn in Bethlehem, the gift Jesus has given us is available to all — to all who, like the shepherds and Leah, would seek his touch. In all of the hustle and bustle of life, in the trials and tribulations that continually seek to overwhelm us, in the midst of the little problems as well as the big ones, we sometimes fail to recognize, to feel, to be open to the touch of Jesus — the touch that would give us hope and peace and love as well as forgiveness and guidance. As we celebrate Christmas, we are reminded that Jesus, who touched the hearts of the shepherds and Leah, continues to touch our lives with his love and hope.

Christmas has a peculiar nature because of the celebration around the birth of our Savior. It touches the lives of Christians and non-Christians alike. Most non-Christians accept it, and sometimes, I think, even envy it, for Christmas is a celebration of love and hope. We remember it as the anniversary when the Lord of the universe came down to earth in the form of a helpless baby. That's quite a day and happening to honor. Of course, to many it is a rather startling idea. Some people find it very uncomfortable, for they are afraid of God and cannot accept his greatest love found in an innocent baby. But our God had a very bright idea in coming in the form of a child, because almost everyone likes a baby. So God, who wanted to be loved as well as feared, made a correct move in this situation. But God went a step further. He didn't want just to rule over people, he also wanted to know them. Jesus did not remain a baby. He grew up, learning all there was to know about the people he was Lord of. God wanted to be intimately involved in every area of human life, and so again God moved correctly by coming to earth in the form of a child. The joy of the experience of birth and being involved in a family is a most intimate and precious gift. We human beings value this experience, but some theologians and lay people cannot get beyond the head to the heart of God's love expressed in the Child of Bethlehem. They are much too logical and are constantly analyzing this virgin birth and Christmas story.

So it goes beyond logic to a matter of faith. It is what some have termed a kind of "divine insanity." For all of us this story of Christ's birth is either the greatest lie ever told, or the truest fact in the world passed down through generations. God came as an innocent child. God came in his power to be like us. This Christmas story shoots right into the heart of all people. As Christians, we rejoice in the truth we have heard and come to believe.

It's Christmas Eve. Maybe you didn't get your shopping all done. Maybe you've been swamped with the business of the season. It's okay. God calls us to be at peace, for the Christmas story stands. The story stands even for those who may only come to worship on Christmas Eve, for God reaches out to touch the hearts of his people all the time, even those who want only to be touched once a year. As we celebrate this night, be confident that through this wonderful story, at some time, maybe tomorrow, on that quiet Christmas morning, God's touch will take in our hearts and in the hearts of those untouched yet by the love of Christ.

The Christmas story stands. No matter how well or how poorly we celebrate Christmas, the story still stands. It's true; God loves us. A child in the manger announces it; an empty tomb confirms it for all eternity. And some quiet Christmas Eve or morning, maybe even as we now sing "Silent Night," the touch will take. Amen.

www.ingramcontent.com/pod-product-compliance
Lightning Source LLC
Chambersburg PA
CBHW071813020426
42331CB00008B/2486